Dr. D. K. Olukoya

Igniting

Your

Inner Fire

IGNITING
Your
INNER FIRE

Dr. D. K. Olukoya

IGNITING
Your
INNER FIRE

Dr. D. K. Olukoya

Dr. D.K Olukoya

CHAPTER ONE

The
DOUBLE
PORTION

And it came to pass, as they still went on, and talked, that, behold, there appeared a chariot of fire, and horses of fire, and parted them both asunder; and Elijah went up by a whirlwind into heaven. And Elisha saw it, and he cried, My father, my father, the chariot of Israel, and the horsemen thereof. And he saw him no more: and he took hold of his own clothes, and rent them in two pieces. He took up also the mantle of Elijah that fell from him, and went back, and stood by the bank of Jordan; And he took the mantle of Elijah that fell from him, and smote the waters, and said, Where is the LORD God of Elijah? and when he also had smitten the waters, they parted hither and thither: and Elisha went over. And when the sons of the prophets which were to view at Jericho saw him, they said, The spirit of Elijah doth rest on Elisha. And they came to meet him, and bowed themselves to the ground before him.
2 Kings 2:11-15.

There comes a time when a serious minded believer receives the mantle of power. The mantle of power represents the anointing of God. When the mantle came upon Elisha, he received the anointing of power.

THE MANTLE

The mantle that came upon Elisha represents the anointing. Immediately it came upon him, the Bible says, he moved. There was no reluctance at all. It shows that the man had good relationship with his parents and neighbours. He gave them a bye-bye party to say thank you. The reason many people will not grow in the

Lord is that they are still attached to their mothers' apron strings. Elisha was not like that. He burned the bridges behind him and renounced his former life. This is the secret, beloved.

If you carry the things of yesterday on your shoulders, there will be no double portion for you. Paul said, "Forgetting those things that are behind and looking forward." One way to fall very quickly is to be looking behind. Anybody who looks back still finds the old life exciting. Some people would say, "If God does not answer me on time, I will go back to the world. The devil does not waste time finishing the account of such people so that they won't have the opportunity to run back to the Lord.

You won't see your tomorrow as long as you live in your yesterday. You should not allow one mistake that you made 10 years ago to be ruling your life now. If you continue that way, forget the anointing because you are a yesterday person. Recognise that Elisha had parents too. He had a job and labourers but he burnt the bridges behind him. Likewise, God has called you from the world, so there must be a difference.

Believers do not go to worldly parties; they don't cook their food for them and do not eat their meat. We are supposed to be strange to them. Many believers don't want to look strange but the Bible says that we are peculiar. Unbelievers should look at you and see a difference. It is time for us to be making impact.

POWER FOR EXPLOITS
The Bible does not call us to come and live a quiet life. We should be causing trouble all over the place for the enemy. We should be acting according to the word of Jesus that says, "If you are driven away from one city, go to another." That is what the Bible says. But if you are afraid, nothing will happen.

When you receive genuine power, you can't sit down. It is impossible. Somebody said that he received the Holy Spirit and now he is moving about like an old vehicle as if the Holy Spirit too had become old inside him. Something is wrong somewhere. The moment you get the Holy Spirit, you cannot do without talking about Jesus, or without praying. It is going to be impossible.

THE DIFFERENCE

There must be a clear demarcation between the people of the word and the people of the world. God's children must be God's children. It is clear. The situation these days where it is difficult to differentiate between them and people going to disco party is not what the Bible says. It says, "Be ye separate." Let people know you for what you are. Declare your stand, make it plain.

Some people say, "Give unto Caesar what is Caesar's." That is only an excuse for them to commit sin. There is no Caesar in this matter at all. What God is saying is that there must be a clear demarcation. People of the world may look at you and say that you are looking dull. It is better to look dull and make heaven than to have the brightness of the world with crocodiles walking about in your legs and you go to hell fire.

There must be a difference. You don't honour every invitation because you are separate. For example, nobody sends me an invitation card any more to come to a party. They ought to give that kind of testimony about you.

In 2 Kings 2, when Elijah was going away, there were many sons of the prophet. But surprisingly, he was still the only person following Elijah and there were many obstacles so that he would not be able to receive a double portion. But God helped him and shall help you today, in Jesus name. Amen.

> *"And it came to pass, when the Lord would take up Elijah into heaven by a whirlwind, that Elijah went with Elisha from Gilgal."* **2 Kings 2:1-2.**

THE PLACE OF GILGAL

Gilgal was where Israel first encountered hindrance on their way to the Promised Land. It is the place of religious activities with no power. If God takes you to Gilgal, He wants to know whether you will stay there. The Bible says, "Avoid all those who have the form of God but deny the power thereof." There are still many people in Gilgal. They are engaged only in religious activities with no power. It is practising empty religion and church politics. **Verse 2 says:**

And Elijah said unto Elisha, Tarry here, I pray thee; for the Lord hath sent me to Bethel. That was obstacle No 1. It says, Stay in Gilgal. *And Elisha said unto him, As the Lord liveth, and as thy soul liveth, I will not leave thee. So they went down to Bethel.*

> *"And the sons of the prophets that were at Bethel came forth to Elisha, and said unto him, Knowest thou that the Lord will take away thy master from thy head today? And he said, Yea, I know it; hold ye your peace. [4] And Elijah said unto him, Elisha, tarry here; I pray thee; for the Lord hath sent me to Jericho. And he said, As the Lord liveth, and as thy soul liveth, I will not leave thee. So they came to Jericho".* **2 Kings 2:3-4.**

He was again asked to stay at Bethel, but he said, "No, I am not going to stay."

9

YOUR BETHEL

Abraham was at Bethel, Jacob was at Bethel and Saul lost all that he had at Bethel. Another Bethel that the Bible calls the house of God was later converted to a place of idolatry by Jeroboam. So, Bethel can be called a place of major decisions. It is a place where you wrestle with God. It is a place where you yield yourself and die to your own desire. It is a place of complete consecration. After you have taken the decision to stop your powerless Christianity the next thing that happens is that you must consecrate yourself. It is a shame to see that most of the powerful sisters around now are old women. Why? What happened to those who are within ages 16 and 40? They would say, "I want to go and see Mama so, so and so to pray for me. I want to go and see Baba so, so and so, to pray for me." I wonder when they too will begin to pray for others. When will they grow above that stage? It is a shame. Instead of some people settling down to consecrate their lives enough, they are busy discussing fashion. They refuse to see the design of the Holy Spirit, Who is saying day and night, "Get out of this weakness and receive power." The Bible says, "When the Son of man shall come, will He find faith on earth?" It is only you that can answer that question.

The most popular gift that people exercise in the church today is prophecy. The reason the other gifts are not common is that they require more consecration. That is, you need to be holy. A lot of people are so afraid of living a consecrated life.

Consecration is to yield yourself on the altar of God. When He says, "My son, come out," all you need to say is, "Yes, Lord" and take action. But when you say, "Yes" but you are still in Gilgal, it means that you are arguing. Elisha did not argue. He moved

10

forward. In **verse 4,** Elijah asked Elisha to tarry at Jericho but he refused. To obtain the mantle of power, you must tarry at the place of warfare. You must fight until you prevail.

CHAPTER TWO

THE
ANOINTING
OF
FIRE

You can ignite the anointing of fire in your spiritual life. You should also ignite the anointing of love. How? The principles are listed below.

1. **Stubborn faith:** These days, people torture themselves. Some wear strange dresses, others decide not to cut their hair, some wear tall caps and some disfigure their bodies. They make a lot of sacrifices because they want power. But the greatest thing is faith. The Bible says, "For without faith, it is impossible to please God. For he that comes to God must believe that he is and he is a rewarder of those that diligently seek him." Many people say that they believe God, but they fail to make 100 per cent commitment. Stubborn faith is mature conviction that cannot be shaken, either by the environment or your circumstances. Stubborn faith is when you burn the bridges behind you. You destroy the vehicle that can take you back to your former positions.

    You must burn off every avenue of retreat. That is what is meant by stubborn faith. If you will start practising stubborn faith, you will be shocked at what will happen. What people are saying is not possible would be possible to you. When they say, "You will fail this exam," you will say, "No, I will pass it, in Jesus' name." That is how to operate. Whenever they told Jesus in the Bible that a child was dead, He said, "No, he is sleeping."

2. **Effective quiet time:**

    For thus saith the Lord God, the Holy One of Israel, In returning and rest shall ye be saved, in quietness and in confidence shall be your strength: and ye would not. **Isaiah 30:15.**

14

"And in the morning, rising up a great while before day,(this was Jesus) he went out, and departed into a solitary place, and there prayed". **Mark 1:35.**

You have to set apart a suitable time each day to meet the Lord. It should be a time when you withdraw from every distraction and be in communication with God. If your quiet time has no life, forget spiritual growth, victory and dynamic Christian life.

The quiet time is your source of strength. Unfortunately, city life is turning people to weaklings. Very early in the morning some people have rushed out of their houses. Some carry their Bibles in their pockets and say they will read it in the bus. But when they get to the bus, somebody else has entered and is advertising one medicine or the other and is making noise, and they cannot concentrate. They would plan to read the Bible the next day, only for them to get to the bus and two persons are fighting and beating themselves up there. So, you must create some time.

You may say, "I have no time." You will have time when trouble comes. There is no escape if you want to ignite your spiritual life. So, you should create time. If you are the kind of believer that observes quiet time only once in a while, you will not be able to grow. Or if you occassionally open any part of the Bible and do a crash quiet time, it won't work. Quiet time has to be organised and done thoroughly.

3. **You must crucify the flesh:** The flesh must die so that God can use you. If the flesh is still controlling your life, you won't be able to ignite any fire.

15

4. **Regular fasting and prayer:** The Bible makes us to understand that some things cannot depart except by fasting and prayer.

5. **You must always share your faith with others:** Tell others about the love of Christ. The more you talk about Jesus, the more you are charging the battery of your spirit.

6. **Develop intense hunger for God's word.** Develop intense hunger for it.

7. **Walk in the spirit.**

As you keep doing all these, you will find that power will come. As the power comes you will know that something has happened to you. When God checks your life and finds that there is no fire in it, He will put it down and wait for you to become serious. When are you going to put on the whole armour of God? When are you going to put on all His righteousness? God has His own part to play and man has his own part. When you do your own part first, then God will do His own. That was what happened at mount Carmel.

Elijah did his own part. He repaired the altar, cut the animal into pieces and put the pieces there. Some people's legs go about aimlessly, visiting useless people. They go from party to party, yet they are born again Christians. Those legs have to be crucified. You better place them on the altar. The arms, head, etc must be crucified too.

God wants everything on the altar, including your money and yourself. Sometimes the way you can know how far somebody is moving with God is by what he gives to God. If he spends much on himself and less for God, you know where his priority is. Everything has to be on the altar. When Elijah put everything on the altar, he got results. Stop comparing yourself to other people. Do not say, "I thank God I am not like sister so, so and so." You are wasting your time.

The Bible says, "Comparing themselves by themselves they are not wise." If you look at yourself and say, "At least, I am trying," it means you are giving yourself pass mark and that is not the certificate from the school of power. God may be pointing to some things in your life, one after the other, that have to be sorted out. If you don't sort them out, He will refuse to do His own part. It is not God's business to pray. Elijah prayed and it was God's business to send fire. Sending the fire was His part of the contract. If Elijah had not fulfilled his own part, the Lord would have abandoned His own.

Now, God is waiting for you and I to fulfil our part of the contract. The question is: are you ready? Are you willing to give all on the altar? Are you willing to abandon all and follow Christ? Or are you afraid that if you become too serious with Him, He would send you on mission now. And you feel that you cannot go on mission now because there is no car, you have not built a house, you don't have many of the things that your mates have. But many of your mates who have them, where are they now? Think about it.

Won't it be wonderful if just your shadow is enough to chase out evil spirits? You don't even have to talk, your presence alone or your shadow is enough to chase them out. This is a very serious matter. We need seven-fold of what the apostles had, not even double. Double will not help again. The apostles died a long time ago and the devil has increased and improved his strategies since that time. We need to ask for the flood of the God's power. It is time to act.

17

PRAYER POINTS

1. Holy Ghost fire, ignite my life, in Jesus' name.
2. Let the flood of God's power soak me, in Jesus' name.
3. Lord, make this week a week of power for me, in Jesus' name.
4. Spirit of resurrection, fall upon my life, in Jesus' name.
5. Let my prayer stones be converted to the blood of Jesus' and locate my Goliath today, in Jesus' name.
6. I dismantle every satanic agenda for my life, in Jesus' name.
7. Lord, advertise Your power in my life, in Jesus' name.

CHAPTER THREE

FIRE
FOR
SPIRITUAL
CONFLICTS

Jericho was that place where Joshua met the Captain of the Lord of host in the Bible. So, Jericho to us now is the place of warfare. It is a place of war against the devil, a place of spiritual opposition. Joshua was tested at Jericho. Jericho is a place of conflict. At Gilgal, you have spiritual activities with no power. At Bethel, you die to yourself and at Jericho you fight because it is the place of conflict.

Others may have religious things and ceremonies but what you need is more of God's power. Somebody could have a Ph.D in Bible Knowledge but lack the power of God. Such a person would soon abandon his Ph.D and run after a small boy who can demonstrate the power of God. You can have all the knowledge you want to have and all the ceremonies but what is required is more of God's power. When you fight the devil, you get recognition in hell and in heaven.

> *And Elijah said unto him, Tarry, I pray thee, here; for the LORD hath sent me to Jordan. And he said, As the LORD liveth, and as thy soul liveth, I will not leave thee. And they two went on. And fifty men of the sons of the prophets went, and stood to view afar off: and they two stood by Jordan. And Elijah took his mantle, and wrapped it together, and smote the waters, and they were divided hither and thither, so that they two went over on dry ground. 2 Kings 2:6-8.*

> *And it came to pass, when they were gone over, that Elijah said unto Elisha, Ask what I shall do for thee, before I be taken away from thee. And Elisha said, I pray thee, let a double portion of thy*

20

spirit be upon me. And he said, Thou hast asked a hard thing: nevertheless, if thou see me when I am taken from thee, it shall be so unto thee; but if not, it shall not be so. And it came to pass, as they still went on, and talked, that, behold, there appeared a chariot of fire, and horses of fire, and parted them both asunder; and Elijah went up by a whirlwind into heaven. And Elisha saw it, and he cried, My father, my father, the chariot of Israel, and the horsemen thereof. And he saw him no more: and he took hold of his own clothes, and rent them in two pieces. He took up also the mantle of Elijah that fell from him, and went back, and stood by the bank of Jordan; And he took the mantle of Elijah that fell from him, and smote the waters, and said, Where is the LORD God of Elijah? and when he also had smitten the waters, they parted hither and thither: and Elisha went over. And when the sons of the prophets which were to view at Jericho saw him, they said, The spirit of Elijah doth rest on Elisha. And they came to meet him, and bowed themselves to the ground before him. **2 Kings 2:9-15.**

YOUR JORDAN

Jordan, the last point of call, is the place of spiritual vision. What do you see? The devil fights to keep believers blind. Elisha passed his own test. He saw what others did not see and when he saw it, his reaction was humility. He tore his own cloth, took the mantle and with it he cried, "Where is the Lord God of Elijah?" And the God of Elijah answered. He smote the waters and passed to the other side. The five steps that we have gone through are the keys for operating in the double portion of God's power.

By now you should know whether you are in Gilgal, Bethel, Jericho or Jordan. You should know where you are. I believe that many days before Elijah's departure, Elisha would have stopped eating. He knew that Elijah was going away and if he received just one portion of his anointing, the problem that came upon Elijah when he said, "Kill me for I am not better than my fathers," would come upon him. If he had only one portion of Elijah's anointing, he won't be able to cope. So he needed double. If he asked for double the anointing of Elijah, we of the present day should ask for a seven-fold of what the apostles received, to cope with what is happening now and with the evil that is circulating around us.

WHEN THERE IS NO FIRE

A sister who did not have fire went to preach somewhere. The man she met in the house offered her drink and she declined. He switched on the cassette player and there was reggae music. After sometime, the sister began to tap her feet on the floor. Later, the man removed the cassette and put in another one and the sister sang a little bit of it. It is very important for us to pray the world out of our system. We should pray out of our brain the worldly music and all the things we learned from the world. They have to go completely.

The man said, "Okay, start preaching," and the sister started and suddenly the man said, "Stop. Don't mention that name again. Who is Jesus?" The sister was shocked to see the man's countenance change. Suddenly the man opened a wardrobe and in it were human heads, skulls, legs, hands, etc arranged and labelled.

The sister was glued to her seat. Then the man said, "This is your last preaching, you better preach it very well."

The sister started to say, "Touch not my anointed, do my prophet no harm." The man said, "You, what power do you have. You don't have anything, even the small fire that some of you carry about, you don't have."

The sister started to shiver and to speak in tongues, but they were powerless tongues. She could not stand up again. The man opened another wardrobe and a big snake crawled out and coiled around the sister and began to squeeze her. She began to call Jesus.

THE UNCHALLENGEABLE VICTORY

Eventually, God helped her and she was able to go out, but she was not herself again. When she came out some people around there told her that she was the first person that they had seen went in there and came out. They said, "When we saw you carry your Bible and went in there, we thought you had power to challenge him." The sister could not talk, she rushed to her pastor and asked him to pray for her. The pastor prayed and it took her several days fast to get out of the trouble.

If worldly military officers are improving on their weapons everyday, the devil will not be that foolish not to be improving on his own weapons. And if the devil is improving on his weapons and you, a Christian, are still speaking in the tongues you got in 1990, you are still talking about empty holiness, empty sanctification and empty salvation with no power, then you need to ask for power today.

23

Jesus told His disciples that they would receive power after the Holy Spirit had fallen upon them. It is when the power falls upon you that you will become a disciple. This can happen to you when you are genuinely born again.

CHAPTER FOUR

DEALING
With The
ENEMY'S THREAT

Threats form an integral part of the weapons used by the enemy to fight against God's people. He has continued to cheat a lot of people using the strategy of evil threats.

The apostles were pushed around. They were warned not to preach in the name of Jesus. But they defied the warning and started praying, According to Acts 4:29:

> *"And now, Lord, behold their threatening and grant unto thy servants, that with all boldness they may speak thy word."* **Acts 4:29.**

I had a visitor sometime ago who told me that she had been born again for 33 years, that recently, she met a member of Mountain of Fire and Miracles Ministries who started praying with her and right from then it was as if she had not been born again. She said that the kind of prayer points the sister called were strange to her, although she had been born again for 33 years.

A GOOD REPORT

She said that despite the fact that the prayer points were strange, she prayed them, and she was getting results instantly for the first time and that her life had never been the same. According to her, this sister who prayed with her did not seem to recognise that there was something called fear. "When you say something is big and terrible, she just moved in and demolished it with prayer."

She said that several weeks back, somebody fired an arrow at her and one of her hands and one of her legs were getting paralysed and the sister came with anointing oil, applied it on her, and her hand and leg became normal. She said she asked the sister if she was a pastor and she said no. She told her that she was only an ordinary member of Mountain of Fire and Miracles Ministries.

Then she said to the sister, "If you, an ordinary member, can be this good, I must come and see your pastor." This is the kind of testimony that encourages us, not that of the one who would say, "When my husband was talking rubbish, I gave him a dirty slap and later asked the Lord to forgive me." My prayer is that you too, will be a good example. Any power militating against a true child of God is looking for problems. Such a power wants to sink in the Red Sea after the order of Pharaoh. It is also seeking to be destroyed by God's anger after the order of Senacherib.

One angel defeated 185,000 people. I am very sure that nobody has up to 185,000 enemies. Any power militating against a true child of God is seeking to fight and oppose itself. It is seeking to receive the stones of fire, after the order of Goliath. Any power militating against a true child of God is seeking to be substituted. Such a power wants to receive what we call divine hail stones.

Any power militating against a true child of God is looking for compulsory and forceful burial after the order of Korah, Dathan and Abiram. It is seeking to be eaten up by worms after the order of Herod and to be pursued by terrifying noises after the order of the Syrians.

WHEN PRAYER THREATENS THE ENEMY

Few months ago I heard another testimony that gladdened my heart. The co-tenants of one of our members came to report to me that since this brother moved into their compound, the whole place had always been hot at night. The tenants who used to attend witchcraft meetings could no longer attend because the brother had blocked the way. They said, "We are just appealing to him, we want to refund what he has paid and he should leave."

That is how it should be. The wicked should always run when they see a Christian. They should be having problems not believers. This was not the kind of testimony that somebody comes and says, "Pray on these prayer request for me sir. My co-tenant, the man on the first floor, is a witch doctor and the other one a witch. They are harassing me at night." In this case the brother was the one harassing them. Take the following prayer points with holy anger:

1. Every witch living in my surrounding, receive the stones of fire, in the name of Jesus.
2. Any evil vessel conveying my information to the evil world, be paralysed now, in the name of Jesus.

What are the principles of praying to get results?
There are many examples in the Bible of those who prayed and got results instantly. For us to understand the principles, we shall study the prayer points of some of such people. They are many but we will look at only three examples.

1. **MOSES**
    In Numbers 16, Korah, Dathan and Abiram offended God by offending His servant. In verses 28 - 33, that servant of God said:

    > "And Moses said, hereby ye shall know that the Lord hath sent me to do all these works, for I have not

done them of mine own mind. If these men die the common death of all men, or if they be visited after the visitation of all men; then the Lord hath not sent me. But if the Lord make a new thing and the earth open her mouth and swallow them up, with all that appertain unto them, and they go down quick into the pit; then ye shall understand that these men have provoked the Lord. And it came to pass, as he had made an end of speaking all these words, that the ground clave asunder that was under them; And the earth opened her mouth; and swallowed them up and their houses and all the men that appertained unto Korah and all their goods. They and all that appertained to them went down alive into the pit and the earth closed upon them and they perished from among the congregation." **Numbers 16:28 - 33.**

2.   **ELIJAH**

"And it came to pass at the time of the offering of the evening sacrifice, that Elijah the Prophet came near and said, Lord God of Abraham, Isaac and of Israel, let it be known this day that thou art God in Israel and that I am thy servant, and that I have done all these things at thy word. Hear me O Lord, hear me that this people may know that thou art the Lord God and that thou hast turned their heart back again. Then the fire of the Lord fell, and consumed the burnt sacrifice, and the wood, and the stones, and the dust, and licked up the water that was in the trench. And when all the people saw it, they fell on their faces: and they said, the Lord, he is the God; the Lord he is the God." **1 Kings 18:36.**

The man prayed a prayer point of about 60 words and instantly things began to happen. Compare his wording with the wording of the prayer of Moses.

3. **THE APOSTLES**

The apostles had been beaten up and had been told not to preach in the name of Jesus. They had been threatened that if they continued to preach in that name, they would be killed. But they defied the threat.

> "And being let go, they went to their own company and reported all that the chief priests and elders had said unto them. And when they heard that, they lifted up their voice to God with one accord, and said, Lord, thou art God, which hast made heaven and earth and the sea and all that in them is; who by the mouth of thy servant David hast said why did the heathen rage and the people imagine vain things? The kings of the earth stood up, and the rulers were gathered together against the Lord, and against his Christ" **Acts 4: 23 - 27.**

> "And now, Lord, behold their threatening and grant unto thy servants, that with all boldness they may speak thy word. By stretching forth thine hand to heal; and that signs and wonders may be done by the name of thy holy child Jesus. And when they had prayed, the place was shaken where they were assembled to-gether; and they were all filled with the Holy Ghost

and they spake the word of God with boldness." **Acts 4:29 - 31.**

What are the characteristics of these three passages?

1. **A petition was filed to God.** The Bible says, plead your cause before the Almighty.

2. **The troublers of Israel were reported directly to God as if God did not see them.** We too should form that kind of habit. Talk to God as a friend. When you wake up and you don't like the kind of dreams you had, you can sit down and say, "Father, when I slept last night, I had so and so dream. I don't understand what they mean. Explain them to me and teach me what to do.

    Report the cases to God, as if He did not know about the dreams.

3. **War was declared against the opposing forces.**

4. **Instant divine intervention was requested.** If God is not going to give you the cash now, you can at least go with the cheque. That is a good way to start with.

5. **They prayed from the bottom of their hearts.** There is a difference between surface prayer and deep prayer. Whenever prayer comes from the bottom of the heart, it yields results.

6. There was instant faith and holy expectancy.

7. They prayed using the standard of somebody who is divinely dissatisfied. You have to declare today too that you are divinely dissatisfied with your unfavourable situation.

8. They asked for divine judgment against opposition.

9. They made an urgent request for the display of the supernatural.

10. Signs and wonders were expressly requested.

CHAPTER FIVE

THE MYSTERY OF PRAYER POINTS

Having looked at the major characteristics of these three passages, let us consider the prayer points. I was not there but from what I can see in the word of God, I have an idea of the kind of prayer points these people prayed. They must have prayed the kind of prayer points we sometimes pray. For example, "Let God be God in my Red Sea situation." Check what Moses, Elijah and the apostles said, "Let it be known that I do this thing, because You sent me; let it be known that thou art God."

PRAYER POINTS

They might have also prayed: "Let it be known that you are God in every department of my life." Or, "Lord, do a new thing to my enemies that will permanently destroy their powers." God did a new thing to Korah, Dathan and Abiram. They broke a record. They were the first men to go to hell fire without dying.

They must have prayed like this: "O Lord, utilise uncommon techniques to disgrace my opposition." They must have said:

1. Let the earth open up and swallow every stubborn pursuer, in the name of Jesus.
2. O Lord, God of Abraham, God of Isaac, God of Jacob, manifest Yourself in Your power, in Jesus' name.
3. O Lord, answer me by fire and roast every single stronghold, in the name of Jesus.
4. Every power challenging God's power in my life, be disgraced, in the name of Jesus.
5. Let every rage of the enemy quench, in the name of Jesus.
6. Let every evil imagination fashioned against me, be frustrated and disgraced, in the name of Jesus.
7. Let every satanic plan that concerns my life be rendered a failure, in the name of Jesus.

8. Every evil ruler assembled against me, be scattered unto desolation,in the name of Jesus.
9. O Lord, behold these powers threatening me,in the name of Jesus.
10. O Lord, give me d ivine boldness to d isgrace my oppressor,in the name of Jesus.
11. O Lord, stretch out your mighty hand to perform signs and wonders in my l ife, in the name of Jesus.
    These are examples of the kind of prayer they prayed and had instant results.

Many of us, whether we l ike it or not, have arrived at our Red Sea situations. Some got there very early in l ife. Some have arrived now; some have just started to hear the sound of Pharaoh running after them.

TRAUMATIC EXPERIENCES

A woman came to me, broke down and cried: "This is d isgusting. If I had known that Nigeria was l ike this, I would have kept my husband in England. Immed iately we got here, he just forgot us and started running after other women whom he brings to the house and they take anything they l ike and go away. The first time I tried to challenge them, three of them beat me up. Oh, what kind of thing is this?"

I said, "Well, if you want to cry, I give you one week to do that and when you finish you can come back." She said, "I have stopped, sir." I told her that prayer and crying do not work together. You may cry only for your sins. That is fine.

> *"Thus the Lord saved Israel that day out of the hands of the Egyptians; and Israel saw the Egyptians dead upon the sea shore."* **Exodus 14: 30.**

35

THE MINUS

That was the end of that contest. The Egyptians sank like lead in the Red Sea. A sister came all the way from a far place to Lagos for the anointing service. She brought her boy who was five or six years old, who had never talked. At his young age he had arrived at the Red Sea. It is like when you go for an examination and before you have answered any question the examiner asks you to bring your answer sheet. You give it to him and he says, "Minus 50!"

A lot of people have such experience. Their enemies start with them from the womb. He had removed 50 marks from 100 even before they became adults. At the anointing service, there was a word of knowledge that somebody who could not speak would speak. After the service, the mother gave the boy the anointing oil and they travelled back home. As both of them were sleeping the woman suddenly started to hear, "Amen, Amen, Amen!"

A MIRACLE!

As she looked up, it was her boy making the sound. The first sound that this boy made in five to six years was Amen! That was how he started to talk. Many people are at present camping by the Red Sea. They find that they cannot move further. They have arrived at the Red Sea! Things were moving smoothly and suddenly, the smoothness faded out. Heaven became brass and the fake prophets began to make money out of them.

A man told me that one fake prophet told him to sell his big house in Allen Avenue, Ikeja, Lagos for ₦3 million, a house he spent ₦11.5 million to build. He told him to sell. He did and the prophet collected the whole money and went away. And that was the only house the man had. The door of escape for some people is getting

36

farther and farther. That is the Red Sea. The joyful morning of some people is bringing in a fearful night now. The nice flower in the hands of some people are being buried.

THE LORD SHALL FIGHT

Some people are under hot pursuit. They are being pursued by dark forces with evil rage. It is a Red Sea. Perhaps, you too have been hearing the battle cry of the enemy, the battle cry of witches and wizards, sounding right there in your ears. I have news for you now: The Lord shall fight for you.

Jesus has all the strength and victory. All creatures, which are living now, which have lived and which will be, are less than the smallest grain of sand before the power of Jesus. When the Israelites were being pursued, they could not fight. They had no army, no chariots, no horses, and no trained soldiers. Everything seemed to be working in favour of Pharaoh until something happened. A voice spoke from heaven and immediately that was the end of the contest.

The Lord said, "Speak unto the children of Israel that they go forth." Then Pharaoh learnt a big lesson: that man is nothing. He even learnt a second lesson: that God can use the instrument that saves His children to destroy another. That was what He did in the Red Sea. The Israelites passed through. The same Red Sea swallowed the Egyptians. All the tests and their preaching did not work as far as God was concerned.

Therefore, beloved, I want you to close your eyes and pray with holy madness like this: "Let impossibility be disgraced before me today, in the name of Jesus." I want to apply a parable from Matthew 22. There was a feast and something happened at that feast:

37

"And when the king came in to see the guest, he saw there, a man which had not on a wedding garment. And he saith unto him, how comest thou in hither not having a wedding garment? And he was speechless. Then said the king to the servants, bind his hand and foot, and take him away and cast him into outer darkness, there shall be weeping and gnashing of teeth."
Matthew 22:11-13.

THE ASSAULT

Notice certain points about that parable. A king invited people to his feast. He did not force people to attend but there was an enemy at the feast. Every enemy at the feast of your life, shall be disgraced today, in the name of Jesus. The enemy who walked in by his own legs became the criminal. Then the executioners quickly removed him. It is interesting that the members of the firing squad were also present at the feast. Whenever God is doing something good in people's lives, a proportion of unworthy forces try to attack them. Whenever God is doing something great in your life, a proportion of members from the camp of the enemy will attend the meeting. No matter how good your security system is, they creep in unawares.

God wants to use good materials. If a person then decides to be a useless material, the person will have himself to blame. People should understand that just as this man went from the wedding feast to hell fire, the same thing happened to Korah, Dathan and Abiram. There are powers like that. The feast is what God is doing in your life, the king is Jesus, those invited, the guests without the wedding garments are the enemies that have come in who are satanic agents. All such agents shall be paralysed now, in the name of Jesus. So this is why God calls His people the apple of His eye, the delight of His eye and the joy of His eye.

Make this declaration: "Evil powers might be drinking other people's blood and wasting their lives, but my case is different. Every power designing shame and embarrassment for me, be paralysed, in the name of Jesus. Any power that says I should eat sand, should eat sand, in the name of Jesus.

THE GOD OF THE SAINTS

All those who have been harassing the children of God are probably not reading their Bibles. They have not read about Pharaoh, Haman or those who threw Daniel into the lions' den. The big truth is this: there is no one who has battled against the saints and is not ruined by the God of the saints.

Check it out. Those who fought against Daniel were ruined by the God of Daniel. Those who fought against the Israelites, including Pharaoh, were ruined by their God. An angel just gave Herod a little slap, not a big one because if he did, that would have roasted him. In fact, we need to ask for angelic assistance today because when God sends His angels, they slap our enemies, block their transport routes, invite special fire upon them, attack them with the sword or give them the last warning.

Angels too can issue curses. They can stretch out their hands and destroy. They can chase or persecute people. For example, you heard the Psalmist praying, "Let the angels of God pursue them. Let them have no rest day and night."

At this juncture, I would like you to pray like this: "Let the angels of God pursue and persecute all the enemies of my soul, in Jesus' name."

39

PRAYER POINTS

1. Let God be God in all my situations, in the name of Jesus.

2. Lord, let it be known that your are God, in the name of Jesus.

3. Lord, do a new thing to my enemies, in the name of Jesus.

4. Let the earth open up and swallow every stubborn pursuer, in the name of Jesus.

5. Lord God of Abraham, Isaac and Jacob, manifest Yourself in Your power, in the name of Jesus.

6. Lord God of Elijah, answer my prayers by fire, in the name of Jesus.

7. Every power challenging divine power in my life, be disgraced now, in the name of Jesus.

8. Every satanic plan against my life, be rendered impotent, in the name of Jesus.

9. Every evil power assembled against me, be scattered unto desolation, in the name of Jesus.

10. Lord, behold the threatening of my enemies and silence them, in the name of Jesus.

11. I shall laugh last, in the name of Jesus.

12. Lord, let my prayer letter result in your signs and wonders for me, in the name of Jesus.

13. Every rage of the enemy, be quenched, in the name of Jesus.

OTHER BOOKS BY DR. D. K. OLUKOYA

1. 20 Marching Orders To Fulfill Your Destiny
2. 30 Things The Anointing Can Do For You
3. 30 Prophetic Arrows From Heaven
4. A-Z of Complete Deliverance
5. Abraham's Children in Bondage
6. Basic Prayer Patterns
7. Be Prepared
8. Bewitchment must die
9. Biblical Principles of Dream Interpretation
10. Born Great, But Tied Down
11. Breaking Bad Habits
12. Breakthrough Prayers For Business Professionals
13. Bringing Down The Power of God
14. Brokenness
15. Can God Trust You?
16. Can God?
17. Command The Morning
18. Connecting to The God of Breakthroughs
19. Consecration Commitment & Loyalty
20. Contending For The Kingdom
21. Criminals In The House Of God
22. Dancers At The Gate of Death
23. Dealing With The Evil Powers Of Your Father's House
24. Dealing With Tropical Demons
25. Dealing With Local Satanic Technology
26. Dealing With Witchcraft Barbers
27. Dealing With Unprofitable Roots
28. Dealing With Hidden Curses
29. Dealing With Destiny Vultures
30. Dealing With Satanic Exchange

43298455R00026

Made in the USA
Lexington, KY
26 July 2015